Forgiving The Unthinkable

7 STEPS TO FORGIVE YOURSELF AND OVERCOME THE PAIN AND SHAME OF HAVING AN ABORTION

YAKOL WHITNEY

Table of Contents

Introduction

"......NEVERTHELESS NOT MY WILL, BUT THINE, BE DONE." - LUKE 22:42 KJV

I will never forget the day I realized I was finally healed from the trauma, pain, and shame of having an abortion. I was excited that I had finally received my breakthrough, and was ready to put that chapter of my life behind me. I was done, or so I thought.

I also remember the day that I heard The Lord speak to me. He said that since I had received my healing, it was now time for me to share my testimony, and write a book to show others how to receive the same healing. This was definitely a, "Not my will, but thine will be done moment," because I was not too thrilled about sharing one of the darkest moments of my life with the entire world. Plus, I didn't want to hurt anyone's feelings. The Lord asked me, "What's more important, their feelings or my will for your life?" Needless to say, I wrote the book.

Abortion is a sensitive topic and is often off-limits for discussion if you are a Christian. We need more open and honest conversations in the church body on the topics of sex education, teen pregnancy, abstinence, abortion, and adoption so that we can help decrease the rate of teen pregnancy and abortion. Studies suggest that 3 out of 10 girls in the U.S. will become pregnant before the age of 19. My prayer is that we can use our resources to help lower these numbers.

Whether you have had an abortion or been involved in an abortion in some way, my prayer is that you find forgiveness, freedom, and healing after reading this book, and when you heal, because you will heal, be sure to share this book with the next person who has had an abortion, or participated in one so that they can be healed also.

Part 1. My Story

Ch. 1. Decisions

**"DO WHAT'S RIGHT, NOT WHAT'S EASY."
-AUTHOR UNKNOWN**

"I'm not supporting you in this!" I heard the words but somehow I could not process them. They did not make any sense. I was pregnant, about six week to be exact. A child, a life was growing inside of me. I didn't understand what he meant when he said he was not supporting me. Is that even an option once you create a life?

I frowned as confusion clouded my face and mind. "But I...." I tried to speak, but my words got caught in my throat. "I said I'm not supporting you in this and I will send you the money for the abortion!" His tone was low and angry. Abortion?? He could not be serious. I had heard stories about other teen girls getting abortions but I wanted to keep my baby. I AM keeping my baby, I thought to myself. I was young, but I would figure this out. "I want to keep my baby," I said. "I'm not supporting you in this! I don't want anything to do with this baby!" he replied. His voice was loud now and even angrier. So he was serious, I thought to myself.

I gasped as I realized that I had really messed up. I was unmarried with no income, no support, and PREGNANT. I hung up the phone because the conversation was not going anywhere.

I was unsure of what to do next. A couple of weeks passed. I finally broke down and told my mom that I was pregnant, and planned on having an abortion. It went exactly as I expected: not good. I didn't have anyone to talk to. I was scared and I was ashamed. I thought of going away to have the baby, and then putting it up for adoption, but after I made a few calls no one seemed to know what I was talking about.

I went to our computer and pulled up articles and videos about teenage pregnancy. I learned all about babies and their development. There is no way I can do this, I thought to myself. That's it! I am going to tell my mom and boyfriend that I could not go through with this abortion.

I told my mom about the video I saw and how the baby was developing and that I didn't think I should do this. "You need to rethink this!" she said. "You know you don't have any support!" It was in that moment that something broke on the inside of me. I understood that I truly didn't have any support. Feeling completely out of options, I called the abortion clinic and made an appointment. This would all be over soon, I thought to myself. Little did I know, this situation was far from over and I was about to make the worst mistake of my life.

Ch. 2. Pain

"THE LORD IS CLOSE TO THE BROKENHEARTED AND SAVES THOSE WHO ARE CRUSHED IN SPIRIT." - PSALM 34:18 NIV

I got out of the car and began walking towards the doors of the clinic. The building was old and ducked off. For security reasons, it had no signs or information on it. The nurse had explained that to me over the phone when I had called to schedule my appointment. "You don't have to do this," an elderly, high pitched voice said. Startled, I whipped around to see an elderly, Caucasian lady holding a sign that read, "Say No to Abortion." I looked around and realized that there were a few protesters there holding signs. I sighed and held my head down. Shame and embarrassment crept over my face like a hot blanket. I really didn't want to do this, but what options did I have? I didn't have any money or resources or even a car at that point. I felt totally helpless and alone.

I entered the clinic and went to the front desk. The waiting area looked similar to a hospital waiting area with white walls, white tile, and hard gray plastic seats in a row. The front desk ladies seemed nice enough. They checked me in and asked me to sit in the waiting area.

I sat in the hard, gray plastic seat and waited for my name to be called. A couple sat in front of me. The man was rubbing the woman's back. They both looked sad.

"JACKSON!" the nurse called loudly. I got up from my seat and walked through the doors to the back. The nurse led me to an older, dingy looking examination room. A second nurse and a doctor stood there waiting. The nurse handed me two pain pills, and a small cup of water. I took them, removed my bottoms, and got on the table for the ultrasound. The nurse placed a paper sheet over me, and I laid back on the table. She then asked me if I wanted to see the baby, and I told her no. "This will only take a few seconds," the nurse said. Her tone was perky and nonchalant at the same time.

Before I could gather my thoughts, I felt a violent rush of cold metal as the nurse shoved an instrument inside of me. I was not prepared for the burning and tearing. My insides felt like they were on fire. I began to cry. "If you scream, I'll stop and send you out of here just as you are!" the doctor hissed. My entire body shook with sobs. I was not even permitted to cry out loud. There was more burning, and more tearing. Then it was over. The pain I experienced was nothing compared to the conviction that would hit me like a ton of bricks.

Ch. 3. Mercy

"SURELY GOODNESS AND MERCY WILL FOLLOW ME ALL THE DAYS OF MY LIFE, AND I WILL DWELL IN THE HOUSE OF THE LORD FOREVER." - PSALM 23:6 NKJV

I returned home from the clinic, broke up with my ex, and went straight to bed. The pain was unbearable now. My insides felt torn and the bleeding was severe. I cried and stayed in my room for three days.

By the third day I felt the full weight of my transgression. The best way I know how to describe it is that it was black and heavy and I could feel how wrong it was. All I could do was cry and ask God to forgive me.

Somehow, time passes by and life goes on. At this point in my life I would break down and cry often. I was easily triggered and still struggled with bleeding. No one knew my secret but my mom, my ex, and my best friend. For the ones who knew I had been pregnant, I lied and told them I had a miscarriage. I poured myself into work and school. As long as I was busy I didn't have to think about what I had done.

This part of my story could easily be called one of the worst parts of my life. Except that it wasn't.

To my relief, God's goodness and mercy was still at work. Some absolutely amazing things happened! For example, my relationship with God grew! After committing such an awful sin, I felt certain that God would abandon me. I thought our relationship was over, but that was an ABSOLUTE LIE! I repented and asked God to forgive me. He forgave me and showed Himself strong on my behalf! This is why it's important to know and stand on the word of God, and not our feelings!

Before the abortion, I wrote and recorded R&B music. After the abortion God showed me that I had a gift to write Christian music! I went on to record Christian music and my very first song, "It's Time." was featured on The Homegrown segment of our local radio station, 97.9 Jamz. By the grace of God, I finished high school and went on to receive my cosmetologists license and an associates degree in Salon Management. I could feel God's presence with me. I could feel His love for me. He would give me divine instructions to complete my goals, and send amazing people along the way to help me. I will never forget how God walked with me and strengthened me through such a terrible time. To this day, I still make all of my moves, according to God's instructions.

Ch. 4. Progress

"FOR GOD IS WORKING IN YOU, GIVING YOU THE DESIRE AND THE POWER TO DO WHAT PLEASES HIM." - PHILIPPIANS 2:13 NLT

Fast Forward, and I'm a whole grown up! God has blessed me with an amazing husband and two sweet little boys. I confess my secret to my husband. He is positive and supportive, and reminds me that God loves me and has forgiven me. I am doing much better, but there is still a little bit of doubt and shame left. I feel like I am so close to my next level, but need a breakthrough. I make the decision to go to a Christian therapist.

My therapist is warm and friendly. She asks me to recount my entire life. I cried as I recounted witnessing favoritism and experiencing rejection as a child. I cried harder as I recounted words from my teenage years. "You will never amount to anything." There was more obvious favoritism towards others, and more rejection towards me, and now that I am old enough to know what it is: gaslighting, it all comes rushing back.

The pain, the abusive relationship, the low self esteem, it's there, bubbling up and spilling out. I'm crying so hard that I can barely tell my story. I say it out loud, "I had an abortion!" It sounds strange to say, because now it's real.

I feel relief. For so long I pretended the abortion didn't happen. Therapy is finished and I am exhausted, but I have hope.

I start going to therapy regularly. I had doubts at first, but I show up and do the inner work, after all the scripture says that faith without works is dead. "Even so faith, if it hath not works, is dead, being alone," James 2:17. I continue to pray and trust God.

One day during a session, I notice that I am able to talk in depth about the abortion, and the pain and sadness is nearly gone! God is moving. I am healing and I can feel it. I share my story with others. I am obsessed with the fact that I am now able to FREELY share my story with others. There is no guilt, shame, or condemnation. I look different. I AM different. I am confident. I am bold! Most importantly, I have OVERCOME. I am healed and I am free in Jesus.

Therapy was the missing piece to my healing. I am so thankful to God for my amazing therapist. She is the bomb. I am in awe of how God uses her gift of healing. I can breathe now. I have finally beat this thing, but wait, God is not finished with me. There is a call on my life to help other women and teens who are dealing with the pain and shame of abortion. He desires for all to be free in Him.

Part 2. Your Redemption

Redemption:

the action of saving or being saved

from sin, error, or evil.

Ch. 5. Preparation

PREPARING FOR YOUR HEALING

In this next part of the book, I am going to give you the tools and strategies that God gave me so that I could walk in forgiveness and be healed, delivered and set free from the pain and shame of abortion. Before we dig deep into the healing part, I want to highlight some points for you to consider before going into your healing process. I call this preparation.

DON'T RUSH THE PROCESS. TRUST THE PROCESS.

Understand that healing is a process and it might take longer than you expect to heal. There is no set-in-stone timeframe for healing. There may be days where it appears you are not progressing at all, and truthfully your process may appear to get worse before it gets better. In those times it's important to remember the word of God. You are going to have to believe beyond your feelings and natural understanding and trust in God's supernatural power to heal you. Proverbs 3:5 says, "Trust in the LORD with all thine heart; and lean not unto thine own understanding." Remember, don't rush the process, trust the process.

COMMIT TO PUTTING IN THE WORK.

While we trust God to heal us completely, it is important to remember that faith without works is dead. You have to participate in your own rescue. I challenge you to commit to putting in the work. What does that look like? Spending time with God DAILY via prayer, praise, and worship, and following the steps in this book. As we spend time in the presence of God we are being perfected and changed by His power. Psalm 138:2 says, "The Lord will perfect that which concerns me; Your mercy, O Lord, endures forever; Do not forsake the works of Your hands. Keep going until you get your breakthrough. Be like Jacob was when he wrestled with the angel back in Genesis 32:26 and tell the Lord I won't give up until you bless me.

BE PREPARED FOR DISTRACTIONS.

While you are on your healing journey, distractions will come out of the woodwork. The enemy does not want you to be healed. He wants to hold the abortion over your head. He knows that when you are healed, delivered, and set free, that you are unstoppable in Christ. So don't be caught off guard by distractions. Ask God for the grace and strength to overcome them, and remember that you are more than a conqueror and that you already have the victory. "Yet in all these things we are more than conquerors through Him who loved us." Romans 8:377.

9

Ch. 6. Healing

"HE HEALS THE BROKENHEARTED, AND BINDS UP THEIR WOUNDS."- PSALM 147:3 NIV

Do you hear that? It's the sound of chains falling off! It's the sound of YOU walking in FREEDOM. Keep reading to learn the exact steps I took to receive my healing and freedom.

CONFESS.

The first step to gain freedom from the pain and shame of abortion is to confess your sin. If you try to hide from it or cover it up like I did, you will not make progress. Proverbs 28:13 says, "Whoever conceals their sins does not prosper, but the one who confesses and renounces them finds mercy." Don't allow the enemy to hold this over your head any longer.
ACTION STEP: Confess your sin of abortion and anything else you have done out loud to God so that you can move forward in victory. We also confess our sins so that God can forgive us and purify us. "When we confess our sins, He is faithful and just to forgive us our sins and purify us from all unrighteousness." 1st John 1:9 NIV

REPENT.

The next step in your process is to repent to God. What does that really mean? The Biblical definition of repent is simple: It means to express remorse or regret towards your sin, turn away from your sin, and to turn towards God. This process helps us because when we repent and turn to God, He wipes out our sins and refreshes us, and if you are like me you need all of that. Acts 3:19 says, "Repent, then, and turn to God, so that your sins may be wiped out, that times of refreshing may come from the Lord." ACTION STEP: Repent to God by expressing remorse for your sins and make up your mind to turn away from your sin.

ASK GOD FOR FORGIVENESS.

This next part is super simple. I stress this to you because sometimes we make this step hard. ACTION STEP: All you have to do is open up your mouth and ask God to forgive you for the abortion and any other sins attached to it like lying, fornication, etc. The great news is that as soon as we ask, we are forgiven by God and He wipes our sins away. Daniel 9:9, NIV, says, "The Lord our God is merciful and forgiving, even though we have rebelled against him;" Remember, it doesn't matter how we FEEL, we are still forgiven. Queen/King you better receive your forgiveness!

Journal Prompt

JOURNAL PROMPT

WHAT HURT YOU THE MOST ABOUT HAVING AN ABORTION AND WHY?

Ch. 7. Forgiveness

"AND JESUS SAID, "FATHER, FORGIVE THEM, FOR THEY KNOW NOT WHAT THEY DO." LUKE 23:34

FORGIVE YOURSELF.

Forgiveness is super important in your healing process. Forgiveness is defined as the conscious decision to no longer hold a grudge against the person or people who wronged you. The same principle applies even if that person is yourself. It's time out for beating yourself up about the abortion. Go ahead and forgive yourself out loud for having the abortion. Yes, you made a mistake, but you are more than your mistake. ACTION STEP: Declare out loud. I forgive myself for having an abortion!

FORGIVE EVERYONE INVOLVED.

If your situation was like mine, you may have had people in your life pushing for you to have the abortion. Maybe you were abandoned during the pregnancy. Whatever the details, I know you were hurt in some way. Yes! They did you wrong, but as a believer you are required to forgive. I saw you roll your eyes, but hear me out. Forgiving someone does not mean that their actions are okay, or that you shouldn't be upset. When you forgive, you are being obedient to God's instructions and helping yourself gain freedom from the pain.

Remember, forgiveness is not a feeling. It is the conscious DECISION to no longer hold a grudge against the person or people who wronged you. After you decide to forgive, it is natural to still have feelings of sadness, resentment, and anger towards the people who hurt you. It's important to remember that while these feelings are natural, you never want to harbor those negative feelings. You want to be in a place of peace for your own well being. You want to be led by the Holy Spirit.

Do you struggle with letting go of negative emotions? God is faithful. I can assure you that if you ask God to heal all of those emotions, He will do it. I used to carry so much anger to the point I would lose days in my room angry and crying. God removed all of that for me. Now I am in a place where I know I had an abortion, but it feels like it happened to someone else! I have forgiven and released everyone involved. God is able!

ACTION STEPS: Forgive the people who wronged you. Ask God to remove the negative emotions. Whenever you have a negative thought about the people who hurt you, replace it with a positive thought. Philippians 4:8 reminds us to think on good things. Evaluate your relationships with the ones who hurt you. Sometimes loving people from a distance is best. We will explore this topic in my next book. Do your part in faith and trust God to do the rest.

Journal Prompt

JOURNAL PROMPT

GRAB A PIECE OF PAPER. WRITE A LETTER EXPRESSING YOUR FEELINGS TO EVERYONE YOU NEED TO FORGIVE. DON'T SEND IT. TEAR IT UP WHEN FINISHED.

Ch. 8. Freedom

"SO IF THE SON SETS YOU FREE, YOU WILL BE FREE INDEED."- JOHN 8:36 NIV

SEEK SPIRITUAL DELIVERANCE.

I want to be very clear here. Abortion is a demonic practice. Abortion is a sin. The Lord strictly forbids the killing of children. See Leviticus 18:21. During Biblical times, the Ammonite and Canaanite people participated in the demonic ritual of sacrificing their children to the pagan god Moloch. Leviticus 18:21 says, "You shall not give any of your children to devote them by fire to Moloch, and so profane the name of your God."

Due to the demonic nature of this practice, it is imperative that you get spiritual deliverance if you have had an abortion. You may not feel like you are affected by the abortion but sometimes the effects show up later in life. It can show up in ways such as demonic strongholds, mental health issues like depression, anxiety, negative thought patterns, inability to execute spiritually, womb/uterine issues, low self esteem, anger, jealousy and the list goes on and on.

The good news is that God has the power to break all of that off of your life. Romans 8:2 says, "For the law of the Spirit of life has set you free in Christ Jesus from the law of sin and death.

Deliverance ministry focuses on tearing down spiritual strongholds in your life while focusing on helping you find healing, freedom, and victory in the name of Jesus.

ACTION STEP: Start by contacting a trusted, ministry professional, who is called in the area of healing and deliverance/spiritual deliverance. Pray and ask God if this is the right person for you. Often, He will reveal to you in some way or send confirmation of who you need to connect to for your healing.

Next, you will most likely be scheduled for a deliverance session, or given instructions on your next step. Be sure to follow their instructions to a "T" and be open to however God moves in your process. Don't be nervous, afraid, or embarrassed. Your ministry professional will be glad to help you, and most importantly, God desires for you to be delivered and healed.

When I had my deliverance session, there was a lot of crying and release of the weight of carrying the guilt around. God took away my guilt and shame and gave me more boldness to execute my God given assignments. When God takes something away he always replaces it with something better.

Ch. 8. Freedom......continued.

SO IF THE SON SETS YOU FREE, YOU WILL BE FREE INDEED. JOHN 8:36 NIV

GO TO THERAPY.

There are some Christians who don't believe in therapy. They might suggest that you pray more, fast more, or try harder when you are trying to overcome something. They may mean well in their suggestions, but these belief patterns are wrong and can be downright harmful. Imagine the frustration of a person who has fasted, prayed, and "tried harder" but is still struggling from a traumatic experience.

There are anointed therapists and mental health professionals called by God to help people get healed from all types of trauma, abuse, broken thought patterns, emotional issues and more. Just like you go to a doctor when your body is sick for healing, a therapist is there to help with healing for your mind. While a therapist may not always be included in a traditional church setting, they fall under the gift of healing. There is no lack of power, authority, or results in the work of those who are truly called by God. I personally believe that there should be a therapist on every church leadership team, but that's for another book. There are countless testimonies of people who have received breakthroughs from therapy, including my own.

I experienced an acceleration in my progress when I began working with my therapist.

Based on 1st Corinthians Ch. 12. I believe Christian therapists have a place in the church, as their healing power is definitely a gift from God that can be very beneficial to the church body. I highlighted some of the key verses below.

- THERE ARE DIFFERENT TYPES OF GIFTS BUT THE SAME SPIRIT (GOD) GIVES THEM ALL. 1ST COR. CH. 12 VERSE 4

- THE GIFTS ALL WORK DIFFERENTLY BUT IT IS THE SAME GOD AT WORK. (INSERT HOLY GHOST SHIMMY.) 1ST COR. CH. 12 VERSE 6

- EACH GIFT IS GIVEN FOR THE COMMMON GOOD. 1ST COR. CH. 12 VERSE 7

- HEALING IS ONE OF THE GIFTS OF THE SPIRIT. 1ST COR. CH. 12 VERSE 8

- ALL OF THE GIFTS WORK TOGETHER FOR THE BODY OF CHRIST. 1ST COR. CH. 12 VERSE 12

ACTION STEP: Your assignment for this chapter is to find a Christian therapist and setup an initial meeting. Be ready and willing to do the work. It may take a few sessions before you see results, but it will be worth it. God desires for you to be free in your mind.

Journal Prompt

JOURNAL PROMPT

WHAT OR WHO IS YOUR MOTIVATION TO HEAL AND WHY?
REFER BACK TO THIS WHEN YOU FEEL LIKE GIVING UP.

Ch. 9. Victory

"BUT THANKS BE TO GOD! HE GIVES US THE VICTORY THROUGH OUR LORD JESUS CHRIST."- 1ST CORINTHIANS 15:57 NIV

WALK IN VICTORY .

The last part of your healing process is to walk in victory. It sounds easy, but what does that mean? The Scripture tell us that the one who believes and recognizes the fact that Jesus is the Son of God is victorious AND overcomes the world. See 1 John 5:5 AMP. In other words, YOU CAN OVERCOME ANYTHING!

Walking in victory means that you receive the word of God, that you have the victory and live a life that reflects that belief. Below are some examples of what that looks like.

- RECEIVING GOD'S WORD THAT YOU HAVE THE VICTORY OVER YOUR PAST, SIN, SHAME, AND HEALING JOURNEY.

- UNDERSTANDING THAT YOUR VICTORY IS NOT DEFINED BY YOUR FEELINGS. YOU CAN HAVE A TOUGH DAY AND STILL HAVE THE VICTORY.

- SPEAKING LIFE AND VICTORY OVER YOUR SITUATION NO MATTER WHAT.

- MAKING A CHOICE TO CONTINUE TO MOVE FORWARD EVEN WHEN YOU EXPERIENCE CHALLENGES ON YOUR HEALING JOURNEY.

- KNOWING THAT ONE DAY YOU WILL TELL THE STORY OF HOW YOU OVERCAME TO HELP FREE OTHERS.

ACTION STEPS: Use the prayer guide, and daily affirmations sheet on the next pages to help you remain victorious on your healing journey. Challenges may come up, but remember you have already won the battle. Congratulate yourself on reading this book and committing to your journey of healing and freedom.

Thank you for allowing me to share my journey with you. God has amazing things in store for you and I can't wait to hear about it. Be sure to follow me on Instagram @therealyakol

As always, be encouraged. Stay encouraged, and stay in the word.

Journal Prompt

JOURNAL PROMPT

IMAGINE YOURSELF HEALED, FREE, AND WALKING IN VICTORY.
WHAT DOES THAT LOOK LIKE FOR YOU?

Daily Affirmations

I AM THE RIGHTEOUSNESS OF GOD IN CHRIST.	2ND CORINTHIANS 15:21
I AM FREE FROM THE CURSE OF THE LAW.	GALATIANS 3:13
I AM FORGIVEN BY GOD.	DANIEL 9:9
I AM HEALED, DELIVERED, AND SET FREE.	PSALM 107:20, JOHN 8:36
I AM BLESSED AND HIGHLY FAVORED.	PROVERBS 8:35
I AM LOVED BY GOD.	PSALM 136:26
I AM FEARFULLY AND WONDERFULLY MADE.	PSALM 149:13
I AM BEAUTIFUL.	SONG OF SOLOMON 4:7 NIV
I AM GOD'S CHOICE.	1ST. PETER 2:9
I AM GOD'S DAUGHTER/SON.	JOHN 1:12
I AM MORE THAN A CONQUEROR.	1ST. CORINTHIANS 8:37
GOODNESS AND MERCY, FOLLOW ME ALL THE DAYS OF MY LIFE.	PSALM 23:6
GOD IS PERFECTING THE THINGS THAT CONCERN ME.	PSALM 138:8
I HAVE THE MIND OF CHRIST.	PHILIPPIANS 2:5
I HAVE POWER, LOVE, AND A SOUND MIND.	2ND TIMOTHY 1:7
I MAKE GOOD DECISIONS.	PROVERBS 3:5-6
MY IDENTITY IS IN CHRIST.	2ND CORINTHIANS 5:17
ALL THE WORK OF MY HANDS IS BLESSED.	DEUTORONOMY 28:12
I ATTRACT FAVOR, RICHES, AND LONG-STANDING WEALTH.	DEUTORONOMY 8:18
I ATTRACT GOOD, GODLY PEOPLE INTO MY LIFE.	PROVERBS 12:26 NIV
SOMETHING GOOD IS GOING TO HAPPEN FOR ME TODAY!	JOB 5:9 NIV
I AM PROTECTED FROM THE EVIL ONE.	2ND THESSALONIANS 3:3 NIV
NOTHING CAN SEPERATE ME FROM THE LOVE OF GOD.	ROMAMS 8:38-39 NLT

Prayer Guide

THIS GUIDE IS TO HELP DIRECT YOU WHILE YOU PRAY FOR HEALING FROM THE PAIN AND SHAME OF ABORTION. TWEAK IT AND MAKE IT YOUR OWN.

Father in the name of Jesus you are (FILL IN WITH YOUR OWN WORDS. MAKE IT PERSONAL. EXAMPLES: FATHER YOU ARE AN AWESOME GOD, THE AIR THAT I BREATHE, THE GREAT I AM.)

Father, I thank you for (FILL IN WITH YOUR WORDS)
EXAMPLES: MAKING A WAY, DYING ON THE CROSS

And now Lord I CONFESS my sin of abortion to you. I had an abortion and it was wrong. Father, I REPENT to you for having the abortion. You said that when we confess our sins, you are faithful and just to forgive us our sins and purify us from all unrighteousness.

I ask that you FORGIVE me for my sin of abortion I FORGIVE everyone that was involved, including myself. I forgive (CALL EACH PERSON'S NAME OUT LOUD INCLUDING YOURSELF.)

Lord, I ask you to remove the anger, guilt, sadness, and shame in the name of Jesus. I release, grief, pain, and unforgiveness in the name of Jesus. You said in your word that by Your stripes we were healed! I speak healing and life over my mind, body, and spirit in the name of Jesus.

I come against depression and mind-altering spirits in the name of Jesus. I'm thankful that you said for God has not given us the spirit of fear, but of power, love, and a sound mind in the name of Jesus.

I pray for total deliverance from ANYTHING that tries to separate me from you in the name of Jesus. I stand against (INSERT YOUR PERSONAL STRUGGLES) and ask you for complete deliverance in the name of Jesus.

I thank you because it's already done and I have total victory in you. I thank you because I am healed, delivered, and set free in the name of Jesus. For you said in your word, "Whom the Son sets free is free indeed". In Jesus's name, Amen.

Journal Prompt

JOURNAL PROMPT

IN WHAT WAYS HAS GOD SHOWN GOODNESS AND MERCY
TOWARDS YOU? LIST THE WAYS AND REFER BACK TO IT WHEN
YOU NEED A FAITH BOOST.

Healing Checklist

1. CONFESS.

2. REPENT.

3. ASK GOD FOR FORGIVENESS.

4. FORGIVE YOURSELF.

5. FORGIVE EVERYONE INVOLVED.

6. SEEK SPIRITUAL DELIVERANCE.

7. GO TO THERAPY.

8. WALK IN VICTORY.

Additional Resources for Healing

YAKOL WHITNEY

LIFE COACH, WOMEN'S EMPOWERMENT COACH,
TEEN PREGNANCY PREVENTION ADVOCATE
HELLO@WORKWITHYAKOL.COM
INSTAGRAM @THEREALYAKOL
AREA OF EXPERTISE: POST ABORTION HEALING, PRAYER, & ENCOURAGEMENT
TEEN PREGNANCY PREVENTION, GOALS AND ACCOUNTABILITY COACHING

EVANGELIST TRENICA SESSION

EVANGELISTSESSION2020@GMAIL.COM
AREA OF EXPERTISE: HEALING, DELIVERANCE, PRAYER

KATESHA REID MS, ALC

THERAPIST
URMORETHAN COUNSELING
256.281.1343
INFO@THEKDREID.COM
AREA OF EXPERTISE: ENTREPRENEURS, MINDSET, WOMEN

FOCUS ON THE FAMILY

HTTPS://WWW.FOCUSONTHEFAMILY.COM/PRO-LIFE/

NATIONAL SUICIDE PREVENTION HOTLINE
1 800-273-8255